SOLUTION

HOW A POSITIVE BRAIN CAN LEAD TO A SUCCESSFUL LIFE

SHAZIRAM946@GMAIL.COM

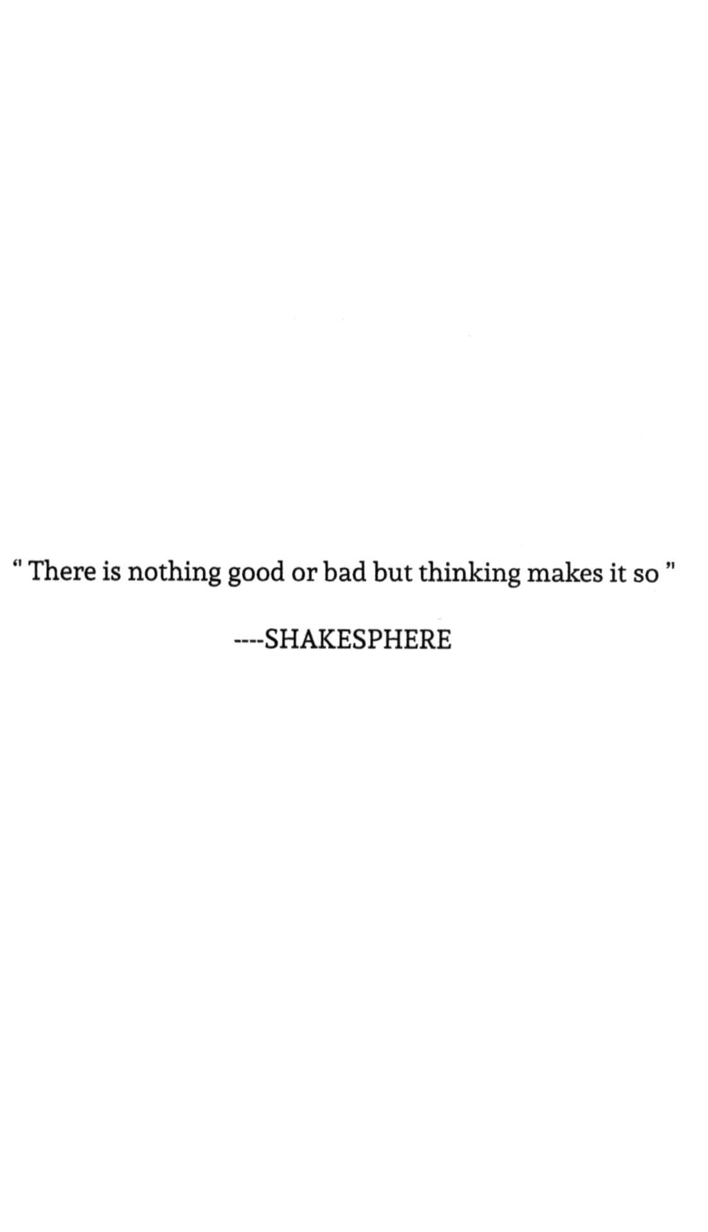

" There is nothing good or bad but thinking makes it so "

----SHAKESPHERE

Contents

Foreword

Problems keep coming in life , instead of running away from those problems , we should fight them. There were some similar problems in my life too. From which i always tried to runaway. But running away only made the problems worse. Then i noticed few things which changed my life completely. That's why i thought that what i have experienced should be passed on to others so that everyone can pay attention to these things and live a good life.

I have written some things, which is important for everyone to know so that they can go through their life well.

1

KNOW YOURSELF

Self knowledge is like a compass that guides you through life. But have you ever thought about how well you know yourself? while we may all agree that knowing ourselves is important, a lot if people have not had the time or resource to really explore who they are and what they truly want. But, this understanding is crucial not just for our personal happiness and fulfillment but also for understanding others and forming genuine connections. If you don't have a clear idea of who you are yourself, how are others supposed to get to know you, Right? so here are some areas you should examine on your journey to get in to know yourself.

- **YOUR VALUES**

Our values define what we stand for. They represent our unique, individual essence and serve as a personal code of conduct, guiding our actions. So think about the things you value the most. Beyond your fundamental human needs, what do you need in life to experience fulfillment? is it creative self-expression, A sence of responsibility. Maybe it's a strong level of health and vitality or being independent.

Perhaps you value continious learning. Knowning your values can help you stay motivated, even when the going gets tough, and it can also help you make swift desicions about what to do and what not to do.

- **YOUR INTERESTS**

What are the things that you pay attention to the most? What piques your curiosity, what are your hobbies? Everything that naturally captures your attention, draws you in and inspires you to accompilish or learn something, can be considered your intrests. And that focused mental state of being intrested in something not only adds colour to your life but also gives important clues about what your true self actually desires. Those feelings you get from doing things you enjoy can be found in various activities and experiences. And this provides your more flexibility and options, making it easier for you to find happiness.

- **TEMPERAMENT**

This is about your nature, character and what influences your behaviour. Knowing your preferences can help you choose the environment, profession, relationship and situations where you have the best chance of succeeding.

- **LIFE MISSION ANS MEANINGFUL GOALS**

Have you ever thought about what your life meaning? To find the answer, it can be helpful to reflect on the most significant events in your life. They reveal a lot about what you actually care about and how you should spend a majority of your time in order to live a meaningful life. Finding the meaning of your existence and why you do what you do can have a huge impact on your happiness, health and productivity.

- **STRENGTHS**

We all have strengths and weakness. But spending too much time trying to fix your weakness only leads to frustration, plummeting self-esteem and a lifetime of struggle believing you'll never be good enough. Focusing on your strength is the true path to excellence and fulfilment. Some people are creative and constantly formulating new ideas, while others are more analytical or empathetic, you get the point. finding your unique set of strengths and the best ways to put them to use is essential to living a happy and successful life aligned with your true self. Now, this does not mean that you should just ignore your weaknesses. Instead, find ways to mitigate them and surround yourself with others who have abilities that can compliment your greetings to know yourself can be challenging, it requires effort and courage, but it is highly rewarding. After all, in order to be yourself, you must know yourself.

2

STOP TOLERATING THESE THINGS IN LIFE

For some people, tolerance is a virtue. It means you're giving others space and not forcing your beliefs on them. However, tolerance can also lead one to being taken advantage of. As they say, life is a journey; and we all have our own paths to travel. We all make mistakes along the way, but it's important to favour and while it's easy to point out when someone else is tolerating something they should'nt. It's much harder to see what you're tolerating and when you need to stop. Here are some things that you can benefit from becoming intolerant.

- **TOXICITY**

Toxicity can take many forms and can have an emotional, Physical or mental effect on you. It could be a person who constantly puts you down, a bad habit like drinking too much alcohol or a stressful work environment whatever from toxicity takes on your life, one thing is certain, if left unchecked, it will slowly destroy all aspects of who you are and for that exact reason, you should never tolerate it.

- **DISHONESTY**

Dishonesty is one of the most destructive forces in our society and it should never be tolerated to any extent. It's a form of betrayal, which is the breaking of violation of trust. If you tolerate dishonesty, then you are allowing yourself to be decieved by others. You are letting someone break their word and promise, without consequence of their actions. People who we often feel justified in doing so because they think they're telling white lies or bending the truth just enough so no one gets hurt even if those little fibs seem harmless at first, they can have huge repercussions over time.

- **NAYSAYERS**

Naysayers wants nothing more than for you to fail . And they will only slow you down . It's hard enough pursuing your dreams and goals as is so choose wisely when it comes to who you confide or share your goals with . Be wary of sharing your endeavours with those who habitually doubt, criticize and put others down. They will just bring negatively into your life. If someone does not support what you be doing, then they probably won't be happy for you. When things go right either the best thing you can do is surround yourself with people who will celebrate your success as much as they apploud your efforts.

- **HYPOCRISY**

Hypocrisy is when someone claims to have moral standards or beliefs to which their own behavior does not conform. It may also be discribed as a double standard, as in the case of a person who criticizes someone else for doing something that they do themselves. It's a trait that strikes at the heart of your values and it should not be tolerated. It's dishonesty and shows that the person does not really care about their own standard at all. Infact, thay may even be using those standards as a cover for something else entirely.

- **EXCUSES**

An excuse is often thought of as a reason, but it's not the same thing. Reason give an account of something that has happened; excuses justify why it should be accepted. It's important to recognise excuses for what they are, a way of avoiding taking responsibility. Those who make excuses are trying to tell themselves that their own bad choices aren't so bad after all and when people start believing their own lies, things go downhill fast. The best way to avoid excuses is to hold yourself and others accountable.

- **TIME WASTERS**

A time waster is someone who doesn't respect your time. They flake on plans, take up too much of your day with their drama, or ask you to do things for them all the time and never return the favour. Every second spent dealing with a time waster is a second you can't spend doing something else. You never really know when a time waster will pop-up in your life, but you don't have to put up with such people.

Set boundaries and stick to them. If a time waster wants something form you, ask yourself if its worth it before agreeing or giving into their request.

- **SELF CONDEMNATION**

When you talk about yourself, the words that come out of your mouth have an enormous impact. Words tend to form into beliefs, which set the factors for action. That's why your self talk shapes you, affecting your attitude and reactions. If you constantly berate yourself with negative language, your brain will begin to accept those messages as truth,even if they aren't . And this can lead to feelings of low self-esteem, which in turn can lead to anxiety and even depression. Try choosing your words wisely when it comes to yourself and remember that its ok not to be perfect. Nobody is.

- **BOREDOM**

If you find yourself bored, there's a good chance that something deeper is going on. Boredom is often a sign of stagnation and lack of growth, two things that should never be tolerated in life. The thing is, life is too short for inactivity and staying in your comfort zone. The only way to get out of a rut or let go of negative habits is to challenge yourself with New experiences and advantages. It's important not only for personal growth, but also for the health of your relationships with others.

- **NEGATIVITY**

Negative ideas qnd images are everywhere. We see them on the internet, watch them on TV and even hear them in songs. It's easy to get dragged down by negativity. Don't tolerate it. Instead of listing to other peoples negative experiences and consuming media that rain forces a negative point of view, turn to something positive. Read a book about overcoming adversity, listen to music that inspires rather than discourages and spend time with positive people who will help lift you up.

- **LIVING LIFE WITHOUT INTEGRITY**

Living without integrity means living a life that is not true to who you are and what you stand for. Like wearing clothes that doesn't fit right. It just doesn't feel comfortable. It drains your energy, fosters feelings of guilt and shame, and saps your self-esteem. Integrity is a choice you make everyday. Whether it's following through on a promise or standing up against injustice, integrity is demonstrsted in all aspects of life. It's about making choices that reflect who we are as individuals rather than who others want us to be, or how we want them to see us.

- **GOSSIP**

It is easy to get caught up in the gossip and rumors that fly around your social circles but you should never tolerate it. Gossiping is unkind, hurtful and usually untrue. People who engage in it often try to make themselves look better by tearing down others around them. Don't let anyone drag you into this behavior.

- **INGRATITUDE**

There is no way around it; Gratitude is something people often fail to practice infact, some argue that a lack of gratitude has become so common place, that we have come to expect it as the norm. We where surprised when someone does something kind without expecting anything in return. What more, not only do people expect others to be ungrateful, but sometimes they actually tolerate this behavior in themselves. Or even worse, they try to conceal their own ingratitude by pretending that they are too busy, livingtired or stressed out to express their appreciation for what someone else has done for them.Ingratitude is an ugly form of selfishness, its the opposite of gratitude and its something that you should never tollerate from yourself or others.

- **LIVING WITHOUT FUN**

You are living out of balance if your life is all work and no fun. To live well is to live fully, not just in body but also in spirit, and that includes having fun. Of course, everyone has their own idea of what it means to have fun, but it all involves amusement and enjoyment, doing things that have no purpose except to bring pleasure. Unfortunately, we don't always have time for this kind of leisure activity, but we need it atleast once in a while for peace of mind and good health.

3

STOP WORRYING AND START LIVING

Worry is a natural emotion, whether its health a job or a relationship, everyone has something that stresses them out and keeps them awake at night. While worrying can be a productive way to prepare for the future, it can also take over your life and hold you back from truly living. just Think about it! How many times has worrying about something made better! Worrying will not change the outcome of a situation. In fact, it can make an Problem seem much, much bigger. While you can't stop bad things from happening, you can take steps to reduce worry.

Here are some tips that can help you worry less and live more.

- **PUT THINGS IN PERSPECTIVE**

Worrying is often a result of taking something out of context and blowing it up in your mind to be more that it actually is. So take a moment to objectively analyse the situation look at the facts and weight them against how things could turn out. Is it really a big deal, or just an inconvenience? Is it worth your time? Your worries and anxieties are only as powerful as you give them permission to be. You can challenge them apart, examining their source and asking yourself if they are rational or not .

- **FOCUS ON SOLUTIONS RATHER THAN PROBLEMS**

The next time you find yourself worrying, instead of dwelling on the problem or feeling like you have to solve it immediately, turn your focus toward possible solutions. If you can't come up with any good solutions right away, that's ok. Breaking down problems into smaller parts is often easier than trying to tackle them all at once. Take each part of a problem one at a time and think about how

they might be solved individually before combining them together into a complete solution.

- **KEEP YOUR MIND BUSY WITH ACTIVITIES YOU ENJOY**

Worrying wastes time, energy and emotional resources that could be better used on something else. How much time do you spend worrying? What would happen if you spent that same amount of time doing something productive or self- nurturing instead. You can keep your mind busy with activities you enjoy. Maybe it's playing an instrument, going for a walk in nature or maybe it's something else entirely. The point is, these activities are meaningful and fulfilling because they connect you with something deeper than yourself, and when we are connected with something meaningful, our minds tend not to wander toward worry or anxiety.

- **FOCUS ON THE PRESENT MOMENT**

Remain in the present moment, and do your best to avoid reading too much into events and situations that have yet to unfold. It's easy to jump to conclusion, based on limited information, but this can cause your mind to run away with itself at a rapid pace without any regard for whether or not your ideas are correct. By focusing on what is happening right now, you are able to see events for exact what they are and not allow them to be distorted with worries about what might happen in the future or with regrets for things that have happened in the past.

- **CONFRONT YOUR FEAR AND ACT ANYWAY**

The next time you find yourself worrying take a moment to evaluate your emotional response to the situation. Most likely, things are not nearly as bad as

you think they are. You may be imagining all kinds of terrible outcomes that could happen if things don't go your way. However , these thoughts are just that, thoughts. The funny thing about our emotional response to fear is that it far outweighs the actual threat itself. The more afraid we are of something, the more likely we are to avoid doing anything about it and therefore, remain stuck. While its ok to allow yourself to feel fear, the key is to not let it stop you from taking actions. Once you master the art of acting in spite of your fear, you'll be able to conquer any obstacle no matter how big.

- **SURROUND YOURSELF WITH POSITIVE PEOPLE**

Relationship are important, and the people in your life help shape who you are and how you feel, so it's good to have a support system that makes you happy and healthy. When we are around people who encourage us, we feel more confident and optimistive about our lives. Conversely, when we surround ourselves with negative people, our lives suffer. It's important to be able yourself around others without worrying about how they might respond or whether will accept your choices.

- **DON'T TAKE YOURSELF SERIOUSLY**

It's easy to forget that we are all human and that we make mistakes. When you mess up or say something. Wrong, it doesn't mean you are terrible person, it just means you messed rep or said something wrong. It can be so easy to get caught up in your own head and take everything you do or say seriously. But it's important not to be overly critical of yourself, because sometimes things just happen. When things don't go as planned, remind yourself that this isn't the end of the world, if something doesn't workout today then try again tomorrow

- **LET GO OF PERFECTIONISM**

You may be familiar with the concept of perfectionism. It's a way of thinking that makes you feel like you have to do things perfectly, and if they aren't absolutely perfect, they are not worth doing at all. When we add this kind of pressure to our lives, and we feel like everything has to be done right, or else it's pointless, we put unnecessary stress on ourselves and we limit what we can accomplish. Let go of the idea that you have to be good at everything. Focus instead on being productive. Do what you can and let go of the rest.

- **LEARN HOW TO MANAGE YOUR TIME**

One of the best ways to get rid of worries and start living is to learn how to manage your time better. This help you make time for yourself and reduce stress. Start by saying 'NO'. It can be difficult, but it's necessary when you have too many commitments. You also need to priortize what matters most. This can mean spending more time on tasks that give you a sense of purpose or doing things for fun, not just because they're expected.

- **ACCEPT THAT YOU CAN NOT CONTROL EVERYTHING**

Acceptance is a key component of emotional intelligence and its important for your happiness too. You can't control everything in life. Some things are out of your hands. Being able to accept this can help keep worry from consuming you. If you're unable to accept something, it's likely because you believe that if only things were different somehow, then life would be better. This kind of thinking leads us straight into circular reasoning and just cause more stress. By accepting what is, we give ourselves permission not only to let go of our worries but also to embrace uncertainty as an opportunity rather than an obstacle.Worrying does not rid tomorrow of its troubles but rids today of its strengths. The good news is that worry is just a mental habit that can be overcome. You have the power within to create a happier life for yourself and live in a State of peace, joy and gratitude.

4

What Happens When You Stop Caring What People Think

- **YOU MAKE YOUR LIFE INTERESTING**

When you stop worrying about the opinions and judgement of others, your life becomes more interesting and fulfilling. You feel free to make your own choices and go on adventure's that you didn't think were possible before. You may start doing things that others might find weird or even downright stupid, But who cares? You will have the courage to try new things, experiment with life, make mistakes and then learn from those mistakes to grow and improve yourself.

If you are like most people, chances are you find yourself caring way too much about what other people think of you.

and it's not all in your head we are constantly being judged in all kinds of ways, by everyone, from our friends and family two complete strangers. Of course, it's important to be mindful of how your words an actions affect others, but if you care too much about what other people think, you might miss out on some great opportunities for self growth and happiness. So let's talk about what happens when you stop caring so much about the opinions of others.

- **YOU EXPERIENCE LESS STRESS AND ANXIETY**

When you stop caring about what other people think, you instantly ease up on the pressure to be someone other than who you are. this can help reduce stress and anxiety. When you no longer care about the opinions or perceptions of others, you actually stop comparing yourself to them. You don't have to worry about what people think of your clothes, lifestyle or habits anymore. You can wear whatever makes you feel comfortable an express yourself however you want to. In addition, your success our failure will be defined by your own standards, not by those around you.

- **YOU BECOME MORE ATTRACTIVE**

That may sound counterintuitive, But if you think about it, the most attractive people don't care what other people think. they do their own thing and speak their minds without fear of criticism or judgement because they are secure in themselves and where they stand in life. If you have a carefree attitude, people will consequently want to be noticed by you. It will also make them feel comforttable around you.

- **YOU MAKE YOUR LIFE INTERESTING**

When you stop worrying about the opinions and judgement of others, your life becomes more interesting and fulfilling. You feel free to make your own choices and go on adventure's that you didn't think were possible before. You may start doing things that others might find weird or even downright stupid, But who cares? You will have the courage to try new things, experiment with life, make mistakes and then learn from those mistakes to grow and improve yourself.

- **YOU WON'T BE A PEOPLE PLEASER ANYMORE**

Not caring what other people think doesn't mean you have no empathy or that you are heartless. It simply means that you know your worth and go about your life without expecting constant validation and praise from others. You are able to say no to things that don't align with who you really are without worrying About disappointing anyone else or making them angry at you for standing up for yourself instead of always looking for ways to make sure everyone's happy, your priority becomes yourself and what's suitable for you.

- **YOU RELY ON YOURSELF FOR HAPPINESS**

You're likely to notice an improvement in your mental state when you stop caring what other people think. You become more present and fully engaged in whatever you're doing. Your creativity flourishes and you have more fun in general since you're able to focus on the things that bring you joy and make you happy. When you can do things for yourself instead of relying on others to make you happy, your life becomes all the more colorful and exciting.

- **YOU BECOME MORE CONFIDENT**

Confidence is about how you feel about yourself and whether or not you trust in your own strength and abilities when you no longer worry about what others think, your confidens soars. This is because being comfortabe in your own skin means that you are kinder to yourself and more confident in who you are. Your self respect grows stranger with each decision that makes sense for you. As a result, you start to trust yourself more and more, your outlook on life improves significantly. Instead of being bogged down by the opinions of others or fear of failure, you can focus more on achieving your goals

- **YOU BECOME INDEPENDENT**

Not caring what others think gives you complete control over your life since you have more time and energy to spend on what matters to you, you can make your own decisions and solve your own problems instead of relying on others for help whenever something goes wrong. This allows for a sense of independence that most people never get to experience because they are too busy worrying about what other people think of them.

- **RELATIONSHIPS BECOME MORE GENUINE**

Relationships are one of the most important aspects of life and they become more genuine when you stop caring what others think. If you have a carefree attitude, it's much easier to relax and just be yourself making it easier to connect with others. People are more likely to appreciate your authenticity and honesty when you're not afraid to laugh at your own jokes or freely share your thoughts and options.

- **YOU WILL LOVE YOURSELF**

When we constantly worry about how others perceive us , we feel less important. We place more value on their thoughts and opinions than our own, making it difficult for us to truly love ourselves. However , when you stop caring what other people think, your sense of self-worth will automatically increase. Your worth is no longer based on the opinions and judgements of others. You will realise that whether or not they approve of you doesn't matter. That much, the most important thing is how you feel about yourself.

- **YOU EXPERIENCE MORE CONTENTEDNESS**

When you stop caring what other people think, your perspective changes and so doed your mindset. You start to appreciate what you have and where you are in life. This does not mean that you are settling, rather, it means that you're living the life you wanted to live and being the person you wanted to be. It gives you peace of mind and helps you appreciate what you have to offer. I know how hard it can be to stop caring so much about what other people think, but the fact that you are reading this book right now, means that you have alrady taken a big step toward being more self confident and happy, keep going.

5

LET GO OF THE PAST

All of us dwell on the past from time to time and that's ok. We are human beings with emotions. As we go through life and encounter different experiences, it's only natural that we sometimes cling onto what once was. Having said that, replaying the past over and over again does not change it, and wishing things we different doesn't make it so. If you find it hard to let go of the past, whether it's the end of a friendship, getting fired from a job or anything, in between, you have to let go of the past and embrace your future.

- **ACCEPT THE THINGS YOU CANNOT CHANGE**

Acceptance is the first step to letting go and setting yourself free. you can't change the past, you can only make desicions today to help how your future turns out. Accept your past and the people who have been a part of it. Accept your circumtances and remember that they don't define you. Bring yourself into the present moment. This is where life happens.

- **UNDERSTAND YOUR RELATIONSHIPS**

It's important to take the time to reflect on your own history without judgment, simply observe. Understand thst you sre not your past. The situations, patterns and people in your life, created your experiencs, they didn't create you. Accept others the way they are. Understanding your past and some of your patterns, will help you recognize why you hold on, and repeat certain behavior.

- **IDENTIFY NEGATIVE EMOTIONS**

It takes practice to learn how to make and identify your negative emotions, try to pinpoint exactly what you're feeling. For example, if you feel jealous when you see an friend with a new person, recognize that the emotion is jealousy and acknowledge thoughts going on in your head that make you feel the way. Don't blame your emotions on someone else. Recognize why feel the way you do, and think about what happened that got you to this place.

- **EVALUATE YOUR WILLINGNESS**

Some emotional wounds can feel so deep. It almost seems like there is no way they can be let go. There may be an endless shadow cast by the pain of your past thst is clouding your future. It is easy to get stuck in this darkness but are you willing to let it go and move on if not try to figure out what is stopping you. The power of moving on, relies on your willingness to take steps forward and how much effort you are willing to put in.

- **LEARN TO FORGIVE**

Resentment and unwillingness to forgive will keep you locked in the past and prevent you from moving forward with your life. try to let go of whatever it is that's holding you back. you will realise that you are not what other people say you are. you are not your pain, your past or your emotions. Generally, it's the negative ideas about our hurtful self talk that get in the way of who we really want to be. Being able to let go requires a strong sense of self,which gives the ability to learn and grow from our experiences.

- **CREATE NEW POSITIVE EXPERIENCES**

Create change by focusing on new positive experiences. Make a deliberate decision to initiate positive change in your life, and make positive actions that will connect you with your desired outcome. create new memories to replace the old one and start enjoying your current life. once you start to let go of negative emotions, you can live more in present moment.

- **DO THINGS THAT SCARES YOU**

Fear holds us back from doing a lot of things. it closes our minds to possibilites of our future, and locks us into our comfort zone. Most fears imprison us and fill us with doubt and what ifs. The more you do to get out of your comfort zone , the more fear will subside. do things that scare you and you will grow and succeed.

- **TAKE RESPONSIBILITY FOR YOUR OWN HAPPINESS**

Do not attribute your unhappiness to anything outside of yourself. If you do, you will be blaming others or events rather than spending your energy improving yourself. A crucial step on the path of happiness is taking personal responsibility. This means not blaming other people for your unhappiness and figuring out ways to be happy in spite of the past and the previous behaviors of other people. Once you take personal responsibility, you will be able to recognize that happiness depends more on your attitude, than it does on external conditions.

- **EXPRESS WHAT WORKS WITH YOU**

Find you voice and share your thoughts and feeling with others. If you continue to communicate what works and doesn't work for you , you will no longer bottle up your emotions. Expressing yourself is an important part of felling good about yourself and your realtionship.

6

THINGS MOST PEOPLE TAKE A LIFETIME TO LEARN

There are times when we find ourselves stuck in the same patterns or repeating the same mistakes over and over again. That's why life principals are so important. They remind us that we don't need to reinvent the wheel every time we encounter a new challenge or situation. As a matter of fact, they are fundamental to being human, but we often don't give them the attention they deserve, until it's too late.

- **ATTITUDE CHANGES EVERYTHING**

Your attitude reflects how you see the world and how you live in it and it determines everything from what you say and do, to how successful those actions are likely to be . if you have a negative attitude, your life will be characterized by the appearances of obstacles, failure, defeat and mediocrity. But if you have a positive attitude, your life will be characterized by more opportunities, happiness and success. your life is an expression of your attitudes, therefore, its important to choose wisely.

- **GOOD THINGS DON'T COME EASY**

Its is easy to get a job, but its hard to find one that pays well. Likewise, it's easy to meet someone you like and even fall in love with them, but it takes a lot more effort to build a relationship that lasts. The point is that there are no shortcuts when it comes to achieving greatness. Sure , there may be times when luck seems to play a role in your success story. But those who depend on luck only end up disappointed. After all sitting around wishing and hoping for good things to happen won't change anything for the better.

There are times when we find ourselves stuck in the same patterns or repeating the same mistakes over and over again. That's why life principals are so important. They remind us that we don't need to reinvent the wheel every time we encounter a new challenge or situation. As a matter of fact, they are fundamental to being human, but we often don't give them the attention they deserve, until it's too late.

- **ACTIONS SPEAK LOUDER THAN WORDS**

You have definitely heard this phrase before. It's a simple concept to understand, but one that is often overlooked. People might tell you things they love you or that they care about you without actually doing anything to show their love or care. They might even say things without thinking about what they are saying at all, they just say them because they feel like they should but no matter what someone says though, if their actions don't reflect those words, then their words means absolutely nothing. If you want to be taken seriously and earn trust from others, then your actions need to matchup with what you say.

- **PROCRASTINATION WILL DRAG YOU DOWN**

Time is a precious resource and procrastinating is one of the easiest way to waste it. When you procrastinate, you're also wasting your productivity since you might not accomplish as much as you could if you just stopped putting things off qnd got going. Those things will still need to be done at some point anyway. So why not just do them now? It may seem overwhelming, but once you get started on something and kindle that initial fire within yourself, you will be amazed at how much more efficient and productive your life will become.

- **LIFE DOESN'T GIVE YOU ALL YOU WANT**

It's easy to think that life is made up of all things you can have, but in reality, its a series of trade-offs and sacrifices. You can't have it all, so you have to make sacrifices and prioritize the things that are most important to you. This may sound obvious, but there are many people who live their lives with no sense of priorities and few limits on what they expect from others. This is a critical concept to grasp, as it helps you put things in a perspective and helps to understand that some things may be out of reach, at least for now. With this in mind, it becomes easier to make sacrifices in order to achieve those goals that matter most

- **THERE IS A SOLUTION TO EVERY PROBLEM**

If You have no idea how you are going to get yourself out of the mess you are in right now, let me tell you there is always a way out You just need to discover it. And the first step inf finding an answer is to stop focusing on what the problem is doing to you. Instead, understand that your problems are only problems Because of how they affect your life right now and there is no reason they have to keep going so forever. Once you get this concept into your head, things seem much brighter suddenly, it's not a struggle anymore. It becomes a challenge, maybe even something inspiring. The trick here lies not only in finding solutions, but also in adopting them into your daily routine, so that change becomes second nature.

- **YOU ARE YOUR OWN WORST ENEMY**

Self Awareness awareness is the ability to see yourself clearly and objectively through contemplation and introspection. It enables you to make intelligent decisions about your life and helps you understand what motivated your behaviour. Once you realise that your thoughts are yours, it becomes easier for you to take control of them and use them to help, rather than hiding your progress. The only way you can truly improve yourself is by taking control of your own existence. By first overcoming internal turmoil, uncertainly and lack of confidence or any other emotion that holds you back from success.

- **NOTHING LASTS FOREVER**

Life is full of both joy and sorrow, good times and bad. The only thing that remains constant is change, so don't hold onto something you have no control over. When life throws you a curveball, It can be challenging to maintain optimism and gratitude for what you have And all too easy to focus on everything that's going bad. But instead off dwelling on the negative things, encourage yourself by remembering that nothing stays the same forever. Bad situations will eventually pass. If they don't on their own, all you need to do is changing something. Good things also come to an end. So don't take them for granted either. Enjoy each day, because you never know what tommorow will bring.

How To Be Happy

There are people in life who just seem to have it all. They are in a happy relationship, surrounded by graet people and living their lives on their own terms. Is it just luck or is there some secret to happiness?

Its not luck and there is no secret. Happiness is tied to our habits, so it's the delibrate choices we make about our thoughts and behacviors that determine whether or not we'll be happy. There are ofcourse, external factors that can affect our happiness. As you think about your own life and whether you are making choices that bring you joy.

9 798888 330111

Printed by Libri Plureos GmbH in Hamburg, Germany